Brain Trains

Liz Richardson-Sugg

PREFACE

Thank you for purchasing Brain Trains. This book is very close to my heart and was written when my youngest son was battling Post Concussive Syndrome and learning to manage ADHD. It helped our family get through a hard time. We used this during our "calming" or meditation times, without illustrations, and he eventually started to request it. As days went on my older children started to ask me to read it to them, provoking deep conversations. Then one day I introduced Brain Trains to a group of students I was working with. They too began to request that I read it to them, laying in the gym or library, lights out. It was in these moments that I knew I wanted to get Brain Trains out to as many children as possible. To help children better understand their thoughts and the thought process in a child friendly concept. To help them learn that not all thoughts are true and that thoughts don't all need to be acted on, followed or believed, that they have the power to choose. These are skills children need to be taught and skills that will benefit them for their lifetime as they grow to develop a healthy mindset. I hope you will use this book with and without the illustrations, both as a children's story and as a meditation. My hope is that it sparks meaningful conversations in the children you are reading it with, as well as, sparking opportunities for artwork, adventure and play.

In gratitude and kindness,
Liz

FOR
sam

Have you ever tried to picture your thoughts like trains? Your brain trains. Perfect trains just for you. That you can control. You are the conductor and you have the power to train your brain trains!

Your brain is made up of important parts and each part has a special job. Your thoughts come from different parts of your brain at different times.

Sometimes they can come all
at the same time!

Thoughts are just thoughts. Sometimes they make you feel good, other times they may make you feel bad.

Everyone has thoughts.

Thoughts help you learn, solve problems, share new ideas and remember funny things. But just by having a thought does not make it real.

Sometimes thoughts can be sneaky and try to trick you. They may try and trick you into thinking things that are not nice, about yourself or even about other people.

Now try and picture your thoughts
like trains. Brain trains.

Your brain trains. Prefect trains
just for you.

You get to pick which tracks those trains go down, which thoughts you want to follow. You get to choose which train station you get off at, what thoughts you would like to keep with you and which thoughts you want to act on.

You control the trains you want to keep in your train station and you can send away the ones that are making you feel unpleasant and yucky.

YOU get to train your brain trains. YOU are the conductor that drives your thoughts. YOU drive your brain trains.

When you are feeling extra busy or excited, try driving your train down a track that makes you feel more peaceful and calm.

When a train comes in that makes you feel like you're not good enough, drive that train right off the track. Derail!

If you get a train that is dark and mean, steer it in a different direction.

Tell that train there is no room in your station for trains like that anymore.

Train your brain trains.

When you have a whole bunch of crazy mixed up trains coming into the station all at the same time...

Pause.

Blow your whistle. A long, slow whistle, like a big breath puffing down the tracks. Take two breaths, maybe five.

This will help you sort out the trains that you really need and the ones that should keep moving along the track until they are far, far away.

When you have trains that make you feel good about yourself, other people and the world around you, hold on to them. Drive them slowly.

Enjoy them and keep them safe in your station, you may need them again.

Train your brain trains.

Trains will always come down the tracks of your brain. Some trains can simply pass you by, you don't need to respond or react to every train.

Coming in and out of the station. Coming in and out of your brain.

Picture your thoughts like trains.
Your brain trains.

Perfect trains just for YOU.

That YOU control.

YOU are the conductor.

YOU train your brain trains.

The End

Manufactured by Amazon.ca
Bolton, ON

42578305R00043